Aztec Civilization

The Culture and Mythology of the Aztecs

Preface

The Aztec people are a fascinating race who've left so much in their time behind. From their battle tactics to the impressive architecture that they have built, they left more than a few incredible artifacts behind. This book will delve into the fascinating world of the Aztecs and how they came to become forever etched in the pages of history. Curious about their lifestyle and legends? You've come to the right place.

This book gives you a detailed overview of the different aspects, from history to mythology, to cultural practices and beliefs of the Aztecs. It will not only educate you about this fascinating culture but also fill in information that may have been missing from your knowledge of these people. It is an excellent resource for anyone wanting to know more about what happened during the Aztec era.

Table of Contents

Introduction

The Aztec civilization has captivated the world since its inception. They emerged on the central Mexican plateau in the 13th century and soon rose to become the most powerful civilization of all time. One of the oldest civilizations in the Americas, the Aztec empire flourished for a little over two centuries and was at its peak when the Spanish arrived in 1519. Aztec society was based on an agricultural economy and a social structure that included serfs, peasants, artisans, merchants, and nobles.

The Aztec empire spanned over 8 million inhabitants across nearly 500 cities. They had a complex network of trade routes that extended hundreds of miles south into Central America. Their influence is engraved into Mexico's culture, language, and heritage to this day. They were a warrior society that had achieved the height of military sophistication when Cortés arrived. Their soldiers conquered most of central Mexico, defeating enemies to the south and north and those who came from land and sea. They defended their territory from rivals in every direction until the Spanish finally defeated them in 1521.

One of the most studied cultures in history, archeologists have excavated ruins from their cities, regions, and even entire islands. Maybe the Aztecs will be remembered by many as the guys who killed many people in brutal, ritualistic ways. Or maybe, just maybe, they will be remembered for their ingenuity. They were a society that always considered the future, and for this reason, they are excellent examples of how to manage resources, avoid waste and create rules to ensure sustainability.

It is easy to bemoan the fate of the Aztec empire, but it would be unwise not to pause and reflect on what they achieved in their short 200-year lifespan. This book gives us an insight into what life was like for these people. It gives us a glimpse into their daily lives, beliefs and customs, and determination to build an empire that would last for centuries. This is their story, the story of an empire that stands at the crossroads of history and mythology, fusing a rich culture with artistic accomplishment and architectural wonder. And it is a story that continues today, not only in the memory of its history but also in the lives of millions of contemporary Mexicans and their culture.

Chapter 1:

The Origins of the Aztecs

The Aztecs were originally nomadic people who came from the north and settled in the valley of Mexico in 1325. They settled on the marshy shores of Lake Texcoco in the ancient city of Tenochtitlán, which was built on a series of islands in the middle of the lake. They became a great empire with an advanced system of government and a powerful army. Evolving from a nomadic culture to one that was highly advanced and sophisticated, they became skilled warriors, craftsmen, and architects, creating their own system of writing (which included books written on amate paper) and a complex system of mathematics. Their migration is one of the most famous historical migrations in recorded history. As such, it is key to understand this history, as well as why they migrated and how they were able to do so successfully. Their origins are a widely contested topic; however, there are several theories:

- **Theory 1**: The Aztecs originated from Cuauhnahuac, now known as Morelos in Mexico. According to this theory, the Aztecs migrated from Cuauhnahuac after that city's destruction by either 'Toltec' warriors or floods (it's not clear) and gradually made their way southward through Central Mexico until they reached their final destination. The Aztec migration from Cuauhnahuac to Tenochtitlan is an ongoing debate because their culture, customs, and language remained remarkably unchanged from the time of their arrival until the fall of the Aztec Empire.

- **Theory 2:** The Aztecs were nomadic people from north-central Mexico. This theory suggests that they had a long history and culture before migrating to Central Mexico, where they met other Mesoamerican civilizations, developed a language, and formed a society.

- **Theory 3:** The Aztecs originated in the Chichimeca region of Northern Mexico. This theory suggests that the Aztecs are descendants of Chichimeca, nomadic people living north of central Mexico. The Aztecs developed their culture, customs, and language while traveling southward to Central Mexico.

- **Theory 4:** The Aztecs originated in northeast Mexico, the Coahuila region. This theory suggests that the Aztecs are descendants of the Coahuiltecans or Tepehuanes Indians. This theory is based on a linguistic argument, the observation that many of the words Aztecs used had a similar sound to the variants of words used by Coahuiltecans and Tepehuanes.

Historians do not widely accept the exact place of origin; however, their migration southward to Central Mexico is widely agreed upon by these four theories. The Aztec migration to Central Mexico and the founding of Tenochtitlan is a long and complex story. It's separated into three phases: an initial migration from Aztlan, the founding and formation of Aztec city-states, and finally, their large empire.

In the first phase, the Aztecs were an indigenous group of Nahuatl-speaking people who migrated to central Mexico from a mythical island called Aztlan. They were originally made up of seven tribes: Xochimilco, Chalca, Tlalhuica, Mexica, Colhua, and Tepaneca. As they migrated south, they stopped at Chicomoztoc, another mythical location with 7 caves. At this location, the seven tribes came together and united as one. In this sense, the Aztecs comprised any migrants who came to the valley of Mexico from a place called Aztlan. Now, although the Mexica were founders of Tenochtitlan and later the Aztec Empire, the expression "Aztec" was employed to specify all Nahuatl speakers within the region of Central Mexico.

The second phase occurred before the invention of writing, suggesting that this was a relatively unorganized migration at the time. On their arrival to central Mexico, they found the place already occupied by several other indigenous groups. None of these groups wanted anything to do with the Mexica, who were, at this point, an inferior social class. Rejected, the Mexica moved from place to place in the region until finally, they were allowed to set up camp in Tizapan, where they worked as agricultural laborers for the Colhuacan, the owners of the land. The land of Tizapan was hostile and filled with dangerous and poisonous creatures, but against all odds, the Mexica overcame these obstacles and built a thriving settlement. Here, the Mexica built their first towns and villages, raised their own crops, and constructed irrigation systems. For the first time in a long time, they were at home, at peace, but this didn't sit well with Huitzilopochtli, their god of war and fire. It was said that he passed a message to the Mexica priests, informing them it was time for them to rise up and establish dominion over the land, as opposed to the mediocre lifestyle they were living as subjects. Following instructions, they sent an envoy to the chief of the Colhuacan, requesting a marriage between his daughter and the Mexica chief. The Colhuacan agreed, but the promise of a union quickly turned sour as the Mexica high priest emerged adorned in the skin of the Colhuacan princess. They had sacrificed her in a bid to make her one of their war deities. Enraged, the Colhuacan royal family decimated their population and expelled them from their region, forcing them to move again.

The last phase was marked by the founding of Tenochtitlan, their most important settlement and the capital of the Aztec Empire. After being driven out of Tizapan, the Mexica continued their migration for a little while until they came upon a crystal clear lake surrounded by a variety of white fish and white flowers. To them, it was a sign from the god Huitzilopochtli that this was the place where they should build their new home. So, they did, naming it Tenochtitlan, in honor of the God of War and Fire. This act, building a city on top of the water itself, was done in obedience to Huitzilopochtli's instructions and in recognition of the sacrifices made that enabled them to arrive and survive at this place. Once Tenochtitlan was established, the Mexica developed the Aztec civilization through an impressive expansion process. They continually went on to conquer new lands and people they found around them, subjugating them and absorbing their customs, traditions, and cultures. In this way, the Aztec civilization grew and took shape, but it didn't happen without a struggle or without cost.

The Rise of an Empire

Establishing the city of Tenochtitlan in the Lake of Tlatelolco marked the rise of an empire, but the story of their rise to power was a long and drawn-out one. As they began building homes and raising crops on their new land, they noticed that they were sandwiched between two stronger neighbors, the Tetzcoco and Azcapotzalco, two independent city-states constantly vying for power over one another. The Mexica understood that they did not have the military or financial capacity to challenge either of these city-states. Hence, they chose a different path: maintaining peace with both parties while establishing the foundations of their new empire. To this end, they focused on farming, hunting, and fishing for their survival and the growth of their population. Soon enough, they ventured out to trade with their neighbors. To them, it was a way to establish good relations and alliances with other groups, a necessary step to solidify their borders so that they could expand into the new lands they had just settled. However, one of the trade routes that the Mexica followed was in the direction of the city-state of Azcapotzalco. As they entered their land and started to trade, they were immediately assaulted by mounted warriors who had just arrived on horseback. Having no capacity for war and battle, they did not stand a chance against this formidable army and were forced to flee back to their town. The king of Azcapotzalco demanded heavy taxes and tributes from the Mexica in exchange for permission to conduct business dealings in the state and on his land. The Mexica complied and began to pay the tributes, eventually leading them to depend on the Azcapotzalco for survival in their current land. They understood that a war at this time would be disastrous to their survival, so they decided that the best option was to remain peaceful while they developed their resources and built up their military.

The next hundred years passed peacefully as the Mexica began to build up their military forces, slowly expanding their empire through alliances by marriage to neighboring groups. The Mexica were incredibly successful at this due to their practice of polygamy. This allowed them to marry into many other families, creating a large network and converting many of these clans into their own. These new allies worked as layers of defense around the Mexica, acting as buffers between them and their enemies. The Mexica still dealt with the Azcapotzalco on a regular basis, sending gifts in return for trade rights with the city-state and the ability to pass through its trade routes freely. This dynamic between the two cities played a major role in their rise to power, and a marriage alliance was soon negotiated between the Huitzilihuitl, the second king of the Mexica, and one of the princesses of Azcapotzalco. The nobles of Azcapotzalco didn't seem too keen on the idea because they suspected a political agenda at play. They weren't wrong. On the day of the ceremony celebrating the birth of their son, Chimalpopoca, the princess appealed to her father to eliminate the taxes, adjust the laws, and grant independence to her people. These demands were a direct result of the marriage alliance, which was unheard of at the time. The Mexica knew how to play the game. They had managed to arrange themselves into a situation where they could control and manipulate the politics of Azcapotzalco without any risk of war.

The king of Azcapotzalco agreed to the terms, ended the Mexica's tribute service to his kingdom, and granted autonomy to the new city-state of Tenochtitlan. The princess became queen, and this was a political recognition for the Mexica. It marked a significant turning point in the history of both Azcapotzalco and Tenochtitlan because it set the stage for a much larger conflict that was about to play out. Historians believe that the marriage alliance began to affect the Azcapotzalco's own relationships and alliances, particularly among its nobles, who didn't hide their displeasure at the tax eradication and newfound autonomy. This displeasure eventually erupted into an internal conflict which led to the assassination of the later king Chimalpopoca and his only successor, a baby, who was murdered by the nobles to be rid of a child that they suspected would be used as a puppet ruler by the Mexica and that could pose a challenge to their own power. This change almost immediately led to a shift in Azcapotzalco's relationship with Tenochtitlan. Their alliance was shifting, the two were now nearing a conflict, and this state of hostility would lead to one of the most decisive conflicts in Mesoamerican history.

The Beginning of War: A New Power Alliance Emerges

The coming war did not take long to arrive and escalated quickly. The council of Mexica crowned a new king, Itzcoatl, a direct descendant of their second king Huitzilihuitl. Still vying for peace, Itzcoatl sent an emissary to Azcapotzalco to discuss the terms for peace and avoid a war. The emissary managed to reach Tenochtitlan, but after a brief discussion between two emissaries of the two cities and their allies, the new king of Azcapotzalco, Maxla, simply said that war was inevitable and that he would not go back on his word. This happened at the same time political factions in Tenochtitlan had begun to take sides, with one group supporting war while the other wanted peace. In this heated atmosphere, Itzcoatl managed to convince the council of elders and the common people of Tenochtitlan to agree to war against Azcapotzalco. They were fully prepared for their opposition this time and began building an army of around 100,000 warriors. During this time, the triple alliance was formed, a powerful military-political coalition with the neighboring city-states of Tetzcoco and Tlacopan. This new alliance was known for its military and political power, the likes of which had never been seen before, and it was seen as a new socio-political force that could be used to counter Azcapotzalco's growing influence. This massive war would soon engulf the entire Basin of Mexico. It would result in chaos and a political reshuffling that would eventually end with Tenochtitlan becoming a dominant power in the region, eclipsing Azcapotzalco's influence completely. The Aztec empire had begun.

Chapter 2:

The Aztec Social Structure and Hierarchy

Many might not realize this, but the Aztec social hierarchy was a complicated and intricate system. It wasn't just about who was king and queen. It was also what the society was like and how it was governed, along with the differences between individuals and their place within the society. While society's government was entirely different from our modern world, its social structure and hierarchy basics remained the same. In this structure, there were different levels of people with different types of rights and responsibilities. These included the different religious and political roles within the society and divisions based on gender, age, social status, and other determinants.

In my understanding of Aztec society, four groups constantly existed in Aztec society for the majority of their existence: royalty, the nobility, the priests, and the commoners. These groups were continuously subdivided within the society, creating a very active and prosperous system. In Aztec culture, the rules of social structure and hierarchy were very strictly enforced, and these rules and regulations came from the Aztec government. While the government was a very complex system with many different intricacies, the social structure and hierarchy were relatively easy to understand.

Tlatoani

This is the highest position in the Aztec social structure and hierarchy. The Tlatoani is the king, the highest authority of the Aztec state, and is usually a member of the royal family. Tlatoani is often translated as "speaker," and they were given this title because they were seen as the voice of the gods. They were also because they were expected to speak on behalf of all their people. This person was not only supposed to make the laws but be the head priest, judge, military leader, and chief executive of the society. This was by far the most powerful role in the Aztec social structure and hierarchy, and this power was used to govern people connected through their own intricate social structure. The Tlatoani not only had to keep his people happy and healthy but also be able to protect them from possible threats. If a Tlatoani could not defend his people, he would probably be replaced very quickly, but then again, the Aztecs were very meticulous when it came to choosing the Tlatoani, so there wasn't any room for mediocrity. The Tlatoani position as ruler was passed down through a strict and complex line of succession. It wasn't just based on who was physically fit or strong enough to take the role, but who also possessed the traits expected from any ruling class in society. These traits included intelligence, moral character, and proper social standing.

To become a Tlatoani, one had to be born into the royal family, but that was only the beginning. The Aztecs had a voting system where they would choose from the selected candidates of royal blood, especially if the previous Tlatoani had more than one male descendant. This was to be able to keep the Tlatoani position from being passed down to a relative that may not have the intention or ability needed to govern a large territory. Once the candidate was chosen from the many available, he was given extensive and challenging tests to prove his worthiness for him to become a Tlatoani. Once he passed all his tests, he would be prayed over and given offerings. He was then required to perform a bloodletting ceremony which, according to the Aztecs, allowed the gods of their people to speak through him and give him wisdom on how he should lead his people. Once he was finally crowned, the Tlatoani's power was absolute, and his authority was unquestioned as long as he lived. This is how the job was passed down from ruler to ruler, and this process has been found to be consistent throughout Aztec history.

Duties of the Tlatoani

There are five main jobs that the Tlatoani is charged with, which include:

- **Governing and maintaining the Aztec political boundaries:** The Tlatoani created, maintained, and provided defense for the Aztec territory. The border lands were patrolled regularly, and those who had the right to pass back and forth were strictly monitored. This was done to ensure that no enemy crossed the Aztec territory without consequence.

- **Administering justice in disputes and feuds:** The Tlatoani were expected to administer justice in cases of disputes and feuds that the lower courts couldn't settle. This included cases dealing with murder, theft, fraud, adultery, and other violations of the law. The Tlatoani were also expected to oversee the judicial system and ensure it worked properly. If something was wrong with it, he was expected to fix it.

- **Maintaining trade and commerce between other states:** The Tlatoani oversaw the trade agreements with other rulers in Mesoamerica and ensured that they were kept. He also dealt with issues that resulted from trade and acted as a mediator between the different city-states. This included disputes over borders and territories and any major changes in existing trade agreements.

- **Maintaining internal order within his realm:** The Tlatoani was also responsible for maintaining order within the Aztec territory. His main responsibility was ensuring that tributes were paid and labor was provided. He also ensured that any people in his territory knew their place and kept him informed of anything out of the ordinary or anything he needed to be concerned about.

- **Being a religious leader to his people:** The Tlatoani led religious ceremonies and activities within the Aztec territory. When the Tlatoani gave an offering or performed a ritual, he was speaking on behalf of his entire nation. It was important for him to be able to communicate with the gods and be in line with their will, as this was a crucial part of anything he did.

Pipiltin

The second most important position in Aztec social structure and hierarchy is that of Pīpiltin. This position is one of nobility or higher class and comes with many privileges. They are usually members of the royal family but can also come from other backgrounds. This position was created to give rights and privileges to those who have proven themselves worthy enough to be rulers or at least associate with the ruling class. The Pīpiltin had multiple jobs that they were expected to do, but all of them had something in common: they were supposed to represent the highest level of Aztec society and contribute as much as possible for its success. The Pīpiltin were often involved in trade and commerce and were expected to maintain their reputation in the eyes of the gods. They were also expected to oversee the tribute system and ensure that their people fulfilled the quota for their city-state. The Pīpiltin were also expected to lead their people in times of war and join the Tlatoani in battle. They also had the responsibility to keep an eye on the Tlatoani and make sure that he was carrying out his duties properly and didn't abuse his power. The Pīpiltin were the only ones in the Aztec society permitted to engage in polygamy because they were the only ones wealthy enough to afford the luxury of a large family. The offspring of the Pīpiltin were called pilliin, which means "children." Unlike other children in the Aztec society, the pilliin were enrolled in a special school called calmecac. At this school, they would learn how to read and write, perform mathematics, and many other useful things. In some cases, their education included the arts of war and government. These schools would only teach the children of nobility, as well as children of the ruler and those that held other prestigious positions in Aztec society.

Macehualtin

The third position in social structure and hierarchy was the macehualtin, also called commoners or peasants. These people were not of royal blood, did not hold a prestigious position in society, and were not as rich as the Pīpiltin. They were the farmers, laborers, artists, merchants, musicians, and other jobs that did not require much political skill or training. They were expected to follow their leaders and perform whatever tasks they were given. The macehualtin were often divided into groups called calpolli, which is a group of families that shared the same land and worked together. Some of the larger calpolli may have had a headman who would be responsible for ensuring that the crops were harvested and sold and ensuring that everyone in the calpolli was receiving a fair portion. The macehualtin were also expected to pay their taxes in tribute to the Tlatoani; these taxes would then be used to maintain the roads, construct buildings, provide feeding and housing, and fortify the military in the Aztec territory. The children of the Macehualtin also had some form of education, but instead of the calmecac reserved for noble children, the common children took lectures at what they called a youth hall or telpochcalli. Here, the children would learn what was needed for their job and also receive a basic education.

Priests

The fourth and final position in the Aztec social structure and hierarchy was that of priests or religious leaders. The priests served a very important role in Aztec society, as they were responsible for maintaining a good relationship with the gods to bring them good harvests and prosperity. They believed that if people were not performing their rites properly or if they were taking offerings from others, this would make the gods angry, and they would bring destruction upon them. Priests were especially important because, without them, the Aztec people would have nothing to offer the gods, which would be an open invitation for disaster. There were different kinds of priests, who each had their own responsibilities within their society, many of which involved directly contacting the gods. They had:

- **Quetzalcoatl:** This was the highest rank of priesthood, and the Aztecs had two of them; Quetzalcoatl Tlaloc Tlamacazqui and Quetzalcoatl Totec Tlamacazqui. Tlaloc Tlamacazqui was dedicated to their god of rain, Tlaloc, while Totec Tlamacazqui was devoted to their god of war, Huitzilopochtli. The Quetzalcoatl was known to be the priests of their gods; they were responsible for taking care of the idols that represented them and even sacrificing people as offerings. They were also in charge of making sure the rest of the priests properly and dutifully carried out their religious duties. Typically, the appointment of the Quetzalcoatl was independent of lineage, but in reality, they were usually of noble origin. To be chosen for this prestigious position, one had to be pure of heart, god-fearing, and compassionate towards others. Everyone held these priests in high regard and were the only Aztec priests allowed to marry and raise a family.

- **Tlenamacac**: This rank of priests was also called fire lords or fire priests. They were in charge of human sacrifice, and although other priests partook in the preparation and execution of sacrifices, only the Tlenamacac could carve out the heart of the human offering and raise it to the sun as a libation to their gods or throw it into a blazing fire, depending on the ritual.

- **Cihuatlamacazque:** These were the only female members of the priesthood. They were responsible for educating the young girls who attended the calmecac or telpochcalli. They were the embodiment of mother earth and were charged with taking care of the local idols, preparing them for rituals, and making sure that they were cared for. They didn't officiate any rituals, however.

- **Oceloquacuilli:** Also called jaguar priests, these were the sorcerers and shamans of the

Aztecs. They have been compared to the gurus and sadhus of India. It was said that they could transform into various animals like the jaguar, owl, raven, coyote, or vulture; if they were captured in such a state, they would be dead by morning. The Oceloquacuilli were also rainmakers and bringers of fertility and health. They were thought to be able to predict the future and divine the location of lost items and people. They also performed many other rituals, such as healing and tormenting evildoers.

- **Tlamatinime:** These priests can be likened to the scholars and philosophers of other civilizations. They were the ones who commissioned and conducted the ceremonies that had to do with religion and politics, such as coronations and rites of passage. They were responsible for keeping a written record of all of the facts, figures, and events that happened throughout the year so that they could be used to determine future actions and consequences. The Tlamatinime also kept records of their births and deaths in the city-states. They were regarded as the spiritual advisors and scholars of the Aztec people.

Tlacotin

Another position in social structure and hierarchy was that of the tlacotin, which is translated as "slave" or "serf." Throughout Mesoamerican history, there have always been what we now call slaves. Most of the time, these slaves were prisoners taken from other tribes or conquered in war or raids. Other times, they committed crimes or were sold into slavery. Most of the time, the tlacotin was put to work in the fields or on building projects. They did not live in calpolli like others and were not involved in ceremonies at all. Being a slave meant that you were not allowed to take part in the Aztec economy because, apart from the tribute or taxes one had to pay, they were not treated as full, contributing members of society. Thus, they could not partake in any of the economic activities that would give them real wealth. As a result, the tlacotin lived in service to their masters until their debt was paid or they had served their punishment the full term.

The social ranking system was very important in Aztec society, as it determined how others treated people and what they were capable of accomplishing. Every level within this system was meant to provide for those who come below them and act as a check on those above them. However, in practice, every subclass was constantly seeking ways to advance and improve their status within the system, which tended to result in a divisive and competitive society that saw many of its people fall into debt, servitude, or even death as a result. Regardless, the most important thing that everyone at each level had to keep in mind was that they were part of a larger whole and were responsible for the welfare of everyone else in society. It was said by the Aztecs themselves that all people were responsible for keeping society as balanced and fair as possible; if they did not do their duty, society would crumble, and the forces of chaos would swallow them up.

Chapter 3:

Aztec Spirituality and Cosmology

For centuries, the Aztecs were a culture of mystery and intrigue. Many things have come to light since then, but the heart of their spirituality remains an enigma still. One of their most mysterious tenets surrounded death and what existed before it. The Aztecs believed that there was a spiritual world before one's birth, and similarly, there was another spiritual world that followed death. They used death to understand the spiritual world and learn about their role in it. Both life after death and reincarnation is part of Aztec religious beliefs and practices.

They held a cyclical view of life, with each individual possessing a purpose and a role to fulfill in the world. The role one played in life was part of a spiritual journey toward creating balance in the world. It was understood to be an opportunity to gain spiritual power, which could help with healing, divination, and guiding the Aztec Empire. The ancient Aztecs were deeply spiritual people with strong religious ethics who believed that even animals had souls that could be honored if treated with respect as conscious beings rather than just food sources or work tools for humans. They felt that they could reach their spiritual potential by living in a way that was noble and in accordance with their society's cultural and religious beliefs. The origins of the Aztec belief system can be found in primitive shamanic traditions of Central America, which were partially shamanic practices of their pre-Columbian ancestors who lived in a hunter-gatherer society based on a seasonal cycle of agricultural farming. The Aztecs, mostly farmers when they arrived in the valley of Mexico, incorporated what they learned from their ancestors into their culture and practices and began to view their gods as all-powerful forces that would forgive and punish according to their behavior. They believed that following the proper religious rituals was essential to going through a spiritual process and expanding one's awareness of reality.

Concept of the Universe

Aztec culture and spirituality were centered around a 260-day calendar that was used not only to organize time but also to establish the boundaries of the universe, keep track of critical days, and understand how various gods and spiritual energies affected life in the material world. This provided the foundation for Aztec mythology. This calendar in this passage is made up of 20 names, each one oriented toward a cardinal direction, moving perpetually in a counterclockwise direction. The Aztec calendar's everyday practicality and spiritual importance together embodied the important idea of duality in Aztec belief. This notion of duality encompassed the religious beliefs and their social, philosophical, and moral aspects of life.

The sun and the night, good and evil, life and death, masculine and feminine, and nature and culture are all dualities that are interrelated in Aztec belief. Duality is the driving force behind these beliefs. Everything that they have come to know is a conglomeration of these two forces: the tonal (masculine) and the nagual (feminine). It is through this balance between opposites that they understand existence. Every aspect of life has been viewed as a reflection of this duality.

The Celestial Plane

The Aztec universe was layered and stratified and celestially embodied the hierarchical values of the earthly realm. The celestial plane was composed of 13 different levels:

1. Omeyocan
2. Red sky
3. Yellow sky
4. White sky
5. Sky of rays and ice,
6. Greenish-blue sky of wind
7. Black sky of dust
8. Sky of fire, smoke and stars
9. The home of Huixtocihuatl
10. The home of Tonatiuh
11. The home of Citlalicue
12. The home of Metztli and Tlaloc
13. The habitable Earth.

The highest level, called Omeyocan, is known in Nahuatl as the "place of duality." It is the residence of the creator god Ometeotl, who is also androgynous. This creator god is referred to as the "Lord of Duality." It is from this deity that all of existence emanates. Creation begins at the lowest level, where the earthly world and its human inhabitants exist, and slowly works itself up to Omeyocan, the top of the celestial plane. These 13 levels are not viewable to anyone except those with spiritual enlightenment or a heightened awareness of reality. In the center of this virtual expanse is the physical Earth itself, which acts as a matrix through which energy flows between the heavens and the terrestrial world. When the Aztecs think of heaven, they do not associate it with the sky but rather with the expanse of space extending beyond the Earth's atmosphere. It is an idea that relates to their deep understanding of duality, a place reserved for those willing to live a life in accordance with religious teachings, i.e., a life that integrates spirituality and materialism into a whole.

The Earth Plane

Below the celestial plane is the Earth plane, called Mother Earth. The Aztecs viewed this physical world as a place for renewal, especially of the human body. They believed that our bodies are parts of a whole and must be in balance with the earth and the heavens. The Earth plane was also considered in terms of the five cardinal compass points: south, north, east, west, and center. The concept of these cardinal directions played a vital role in the Aztec universe. It encompassed everything from their ideas about time and space to their religious rituals that were performed on specific dates. Their profound understanding of the Earth's geography and complex mathematics helped them develop calendars that were essential to their culture. They understood that the world was round, which is why their concept of time was based on the sun and its movements across the solar disc. From the center to the four corners of the globe is an axis upon which all things in the universe are defined. It is where life begins and ends, with many physical and spiritual qualities that promote and inhibit life on Earth.

Each direction had its own deity and symbols, as well as its own color and attributes. The East is associated with Tlapallan, which is symbolized by a reed because it was associated with the god of vegetation and renewal, Xipe Totec. Tezcatlipoca was the god of the North. He ruled over Mictlampa, the region of death. The god of war and the sun, Huitzilopochtli, was in charge of the South, where the sun dies every night and is reborn every morning. Quetzalcoatl, the god of the wind, ruled the West. It was symbolized by a house or calli. In the center of the world was the sacred temple of Tenochtitlan, corresponding to the idea of cemanahuac, the belief that the ancestral homeland was a region surrounded by water. Here, the life force of all things is renewed, and the gods are propitiated.

This reveals much about Aztec astronomy and cosmovision. They were idealists, as opposed to the empirical, rationalist philosophy that existed in the other civilizations of Mesoamerica. Aztec timekeeping was extraordinarily precise, and their development of the calendar was reflective of their mystical, idealistic view of the universe. To them, the universe was governed by the duality of good and evil, which causes order and chaos, life and death. The earthly world at large was also viewed as a manifestation of duality. The sun is a source of light and heat but also warms us. The rain that falls upon us nourishes life in the form of plants, but it also kills the plants that we eat so that others may grow. Evil is manifested in the form of darkness and death, yet it is produced by those who are good and virtuous. Opposites mirror each other and create balance in an ordered universe.

The Underworld

The Aztecs, like the other Mesoamerican civilizations, believed that death was not the end of life. They believed in an underworld ruled by Mictlante-cuhtli, the god of death. This place was believed to be made up of nine distinct levels that could be divided into two parts: the journey and the destinations. For the "journey," the levels included the location where one could cross the water, the place of the hills, the mountain of obsidian, the location of the obsidian wind, and the location of the banners. These plac-es were the path that one took to enter Mictlan, and it was believed to be a 4-year journey. For the "destinations," the levels included the place where those who do not die in battle go, the place where those who die from disease go, the lonely place, and finally, Mictlan. Mictlan was a place that was neither light nor dark but somewhere in between. It was believed that Mictlan was a land of sorrow and a place where one could not rest. It was a place of no return.

The Aztec Calendar

The Aztec calendar is the most extensively documented Mesoamerican calendar and the only pre-Columbian calendar system to have survived intact. It was probably derived from a number of sources, including the agricultural cycles of the Maya and other neighboring cultures, as well as celestial observations and mathematical computations. Like their beliefs about time in general, their understanding of time in relation to their calendar is cyclical; they believed that time was analogous to a wheel that turns forward periodically, like the sun rising and falling in the sky. Time, to them, was composed of three cycles: the 260-day cycle, the 365-day cycle, and the 52-year cycle. Each of these cycles had its own deities and calendars.

The 260-day Sacred Round, or Tonalpohualli, was probably the most important calendar for most Aztecs because it regulated their lives on a daily basis. The calendar consisted of 20-day "months" with 4 weeks and 5 unlucky days at the end of the year called Nemontemi. This is what the Aztecs referred to as their "vague year." The days of each month were numbered from 1-13, and 0 for the five unlucky days at the end of the year. The 365-day secular cycle, or Xiuhpohualli, was based on a solar calendar that consisted of 18 months with 20 days per month and 5 unlucky days at the end of the year. It was an agricultural calendar with ceremonies to mark the changing seasons. The 52-year cycle or Calendar Round was created by combining the 365-day and 260-day cycles every 52 years. This calendar was also a combination of solar and agricultural calendars since it was based on the solar year but also had agricultural significance. It could be compared to a century because it had a new solar year which marked the 52-year cycle. It was believed that the 52-year calendar cycle was a way to keep the solar and agricultural calendars in sync and was associated with the flight of the sun.

The Five Suns

The Aztec calendar also contained evidence of four previous worlds, according to Aztec mythology and the Sun Stone, which provides a history of what happened in those previous worlds. Each world corresponded with a period on the calendar and a deity and particular inhabitants of the earth at each time. In addition, each world was associated with one of the four elements: earth, water, fire, and wind, and the demise of each one would be dictated by its governing element. Previous worlds, commonly referred to as "suns," were all generated out of destruction. Each world was extinguished due to a natural catastrophe that was caused by a fight between the two opposing gods, Quetzalcoatl, depicting light, growth, and life, and Tezcatlipoca, symbolizing war and darkness. Each collapse was caused by the sun's chief element and would destroy the world and all who lived in it. However, the pain and destruction of the past led to a new and better world where people live more peacefully than ever before. The four previous suns were the age of the earth or jaguar, the age of the wind or air, the age of fire, and the age of water. After the crumbling of every world, Quetzalcoatl and Tezcatlipoca were entrusted with repairing the disrupted cosmic order together, with the winner of the battle presiding over the next age.

The first world, the age of the earth, was dominated by Tezcatlipoca and populated by giants. Tezcatlipoca's defeat by Quetzalcoatl resulted in the sun being extinguished, and Tezcatlipoca, now a jaguar, emerged from the sea alongside a pack of deadly jaguars. They killed the giants that roamed the Earth and ended the first age. Quetzalcoatl won a decisive victory over Tezcatlipoca and therefore took control of the second world, the wind age., but was eventually overthrown by Tezcatlipoca, bringing about the end of that age by a hurricane. The third world was presided over by Tlaloc, the rain god, and once again, Quetzalcoatl destroyed the world, this time through fire from the sky. Tlaloc's sister, Chalchiucue, governed the fourth world. This age of water was obliterated by a deluge, in which the ensuing flood eliminated everything. Consequently, all the inhabitants of that previous world became fish. After the flood that ended the fourth world, a new age, a sun of movement, was created.

The Aztecs believed that the fifth age would come to an end on a day they called "nahui-ollin" due to earthquakes.

The Aztecs, and even the Mayans, used astrology as a method of interpreting celestial events in order to predict future events. The movement of the stars, planets, and other celestial bodies indicated human destiny. They believed the universe was a place in which all living things are connected, including humans, a place where survival depended on respecting and understanding this connection and the dualities of life and nature. Astrology, therefore, was the science by which the Aztecs could interpret the universe and improve their lives by understanding how they fit into it. Through this practice, they understood their roles as active participants in their spiritual development. While they were known to be violent, they also possessed a rich spiritual life dependent on the equilibrium between life and death, a concept that permeated every aspect of their culture. Their belief as to how this balance was maintained through their interaction with the universe is evidenced in their use of their calendar. The heavens and earth both played active roles in their Mesoamerican cosmology. The Aztecs found themselves fortunate to live in a world where the divine and natural worlds were one, with the power of knowledge within each.

Chapter 4:

The Aztec Pantheon

The Aztecs practiced a polytheistic religion and had a large number of gods and goddesses. Every city, town, and family had a corresponding god. In addition, every aspect of the deity was depicted according to the combination of plant, human, and animal traits. The Aztec gods embodied concepts like duality and polytheism and were vital to the connection between humans, nature, and gods. Despite the Aztec religion being very complex and regarded as polytheistic, there was also a certain tendency toward abstract monotheism, the belief in a single primordial deity. For example, the Aztec poets and philosophers often referred to the primordial god Ometeotl as the god of duality, Ipalnemoani, the life-giver, or Tloque Nahuaque, the omnipresent one, or Moyocoyani, the one with autonomy or the self-inventor. Although Ometeotl was, at certain times, called Xiuhteuctli-Huehueteotl, Tezcatlipoca, and Tonatiuh, it was understood that they all represented the foremost manifestations of the supreme god. Despite being all-knowing and eternal, this supreme deity was regarded as remote and distant from the world of men and so sent other gods to mediate the affairs of humans. These gods were benevolent and powerful in many ways but were also vulnerable to the limitations of the earthly realm. They could be motivated by their whims or passions. They could get hurt or maimed. They could be debilitated, and they could even die.

Aztec gods were a complex system of deities with kinship bonds. Although they were immortal and could exist for eternity, that did not protect them from dying and reincarnating an infinite amount of times. They had superhuman powers and resided in the different levels of heaven and the underworld, as well as on Earth. They could be summoned instantly at many different locations, and when summoned, they could appear in diverse ways, often through fantastic visions, in dreams, or camouflaged as animals. The Aztec gods were the foundation of Aztec civilization and became so important that they affected everything, including warfare, agriculture, and architecture. They were responsible for the cosmic order and all the elements that kept it in balance, the change of seasons, and the cycles of time. All aspects of Aztec culture were constructed around the central figures of their gods, and it was in the interrelatedness between these gods that the meaning and purpose of life were found.

The gods of this ancient religion were both kind and cruel. They could be benevolent or arbitrary, provident, or maleficent. Their dual nature gave them their dynamism and vitality, for they were never static, never conceptualized in terms of abstract morality. This allowed them to shift from one mode to another, meeting the needs of the moment and still remaining flexible, receptive, and alive. In their search for harmony between their dual nature, they could intervene in human affairs and manipulate them, giving them an almost human dimension. As a result, the Aztec gods were complicated, fascinating, unpredictable, and extreme in their actions.

The Aztec Pantheon

The Aztec pantheon or theology encompassed many male and female deities, representing specific elements and the ramifications of human life. The majority of them were associated with one of three principles: Provident and creative deities, deities of agriculture, human fertility and pleasure, and deities sought after for their ability to preserve the world but need human conflict and war to replenish their power.

Provident and Creative Deities

- Ometeotl, the Lord of duality, the supreme being.

- Tezcatlipoca, the limitless god, and deity of the night sky.

- Quetzalcoatl, the plumed serpent.

- Xiuhtecuhtli, the Lord of fire.

- Yacatecuhtli, the god of commerce, travelers, and merchants.

Deities of agriculture, human fertility, and pleasure:

- Tlaloc, the god of rain.

- Ehecatl-Quetzalcoatl, the plumed serpent, and god of wind.

- Xochipilli, the prince of flowers, art, and joy.

- Xipe Totec, the flayed god of vegetation and harvest.

- Cinteotl, the god of maize

- Metztli, the deity of the night, the moon, and farmers.

- Teteoinnan, the universal mother of the gods.

Deities sought after for their ability to preserve the world but need human conflict and war to replenish their power:

- Tonatiuh, the shining one, god of the daytime sky.

- Huitzilopochtli, god of war, human sacrifice, and the sun.

- Mixcoatl, god of the stars, heavens, and the milky way.

- Tlahuizcalpantecuhtli, the morning star, the deity of Venus.

- Mictlantecuhtli, god of the underworld.

The Major Aztec Deities

- **Chalchiuhtlicue:** Goddess of water, lakes, rivers, seas, and streams. She is sometimes depicted as a young woman wearing or carrying a star-tipped spear or a serpent. She is associated with waves, ripples, and foam and lives in the primordial ocean surrounding the earth. Her symbol is a crescent moon with stars and water drops on it. Her colors are blue, as the color of water; white, as the foam of waves; and green, to symbolize the vegetation in lakes and rivers. She is revered as the patroness of fishermen.

- **Cinteotl:** God of maize and all things agricultural; this deity is known as The Old One. He is depicted as an old man dressed in the traditional costume of an Aztec nobleman: a knee-length cotton shirt, a mantle, and a large headdress. On occasion, he is also represented as a jaguar or having the body of a jaguar with the head of an eagle and carrying maize cobs and knives. He is also associated with fertility, especially male sexual potency. His symbol is the maize cob with a cross on top, and he is acknowledged as the bestower of human fertility, life, and food. His color is yellow, and he is associated with the village, crossed sticks or poles that represent the joining of two huts and symbolize the duality in all things, male and female, night and day, earth and sky.

- **Huitzilopochtli**: God of war and the sun, hero of human sacrifice, and warrior, Huitzilopochtli is often depicted as a hummingbird or an eagle. The Aztecs believed that he was the leader of the southern forces and would lead them to victory in war. His symbol is a feather-covered spear, which he generally carried and wore on his back. He also carries a shield representing the sun and its light, and his headdress is adorned with eagles and snakes, which are symbols of war.

- **Metztli**: Goddess of the moon and queen of the stars. She is depicted as a woman with a round face, large eyes, and high cheekbones. One of her symbols was her owl tail that she used to cover herself at night. She is associated with fertility, moon cycles, and destiny, as well as with bats, which symbolize the nighttime cycle of the moon. Her colors are white and red, colors associated with the moon.

- **Mictlantecuhtli**: Lord of the underworld, ruler of the dead; Mictlantecuhtli is the Lord of the dead and king of Mictlan, the lowest and northernmost section of the underworld. He is usually depicted as a skeleton covered with a black shroud and wearing an ornate skirt made from human bones or flayed skin. His wife is Mictecacihuatl, who rules over Mictlan, and his symbol is a skull. He is associated with death, the color yellow, and darkness. He is acknowledged as the bestower of all that has been, that is, and that will be. Artifacts of Mictlantecuhtli show skeletons or skulls in various stages of decay, with rotting flesh and bones dripping with blood.

- **Mixcoatl:** Also called the Red Tezcatlipoca, this god of hunting and gathering was a patron of the people and ruler of the heavens.

He was depicted as a young man with a bow, arrows, and a quiver full of feathers, sometimes decorated with shells. He is associated with the souls of dead warriors who die on the battlefield and go to live in the sky as shooting stars. His symbol is a black mask that covers his face, and his color is brown. He was worshiped primarily by commoners during agricultural seasons to provide them with food and safe passage through forests.

- **Ometeotl:** Lord of duality, supreme being, Ometeotl, was the name given to the supreme deity by the early political-religious leaders of the Aztecs. He was addressed with two names: Ome (the first) and teotl (god). He was also known as Ometecuhtli, meaning the god of life. He was considered to be the source of the world, its duality, and motion. However, despite his supreme status, he was rarely mentioned in rituals or historical records. It is believed that he gave rise to the primordial deities Tlaloc and Quetzalcoatl. He is the god of creation, the exterior, and the interior, the origin of everything in existence. He has no gender or physical body, being neither male nor female. He is a concept without form or limits. His symbol is a human footprint and is regarded as the bestower of order and balance in the universe. He is often associated with the colors red, white, and black.

- **Quetzalcoatl:** The Plumed serpent, a creator deity and cultural hero credited with the invention of books, astrology, the calendar, astronomy, and the arts. He was known as the feathered snake and was associated with wind, the dawn, Venus, and serpents. Quetzalcoatl was one of the most important deities in Aztec religion due to his role as a creator god and because of his direct association with life. He is often depicted as a snake with feathers or as a man wearing a mask depicting this creature. In one myth, it is believed that he required many human sacrifices to allow him to breathe while in captivity. When he eventually escaped, he changed himself into an eagle that ate all but one of his captors.

- **Teteoinnan:** She was the goddess of fertility, women, and the earth. Due to her strong ties with agriculture, pregnancy, childbirth, and medicine, she was believed to be the personification of the earth itself in the form of a fertility goddess. She is depicted as a pregnant woman wearing a skirt of writhing snakes, sometimes with her brow adorned by two prominent horns that symbolize the life-giving force of corn. She was worshiped as the sacred mother of all living things and the foundation of all creation.

- **Tlaloc:** God of rain, lightning, and thunder and the god of fertility. He was one of the most prominent deities in the Aztec pantheon due to his association with rain and fertility. He is often represented as a human with a monstrous head wearing an enormous, elaborate headdress. In his hand, he holds a gourd or urn filled with water used in rituals. His symbol is a rain cloud, and he is associated with the colors green and blue.

- **Tlazolteotl:** Goddess of salt, lust, and purification, Tlazolteotl is depicted as an old woman with a broomstick in her hand. She is considered the patroness of prostitutes, a goddess of lust, and the god of purification. She is often depicted wearing a necklace of human teeth on her headdress, which symbolizes her role as the patroness of prostitutes. Her symbol is a mirror, and she is associated with the color red, the color of purification and redemption.

- **Tezcatlipoca:** God of the night, death, and rebirth; Tezcatlipoca was believed to be the ruler of the underworld through his position as Lord of the east. He was thought to be a god of duality (heaven and earth) and masculinity. In Aztec mythology, he was often portrayed as a snake or jaguar wearing a mask and cloak. He was sometimes portrayed as wielding a spear with a human head at its end, representing the double-edged nature of man, who kills to preserve life and dies to preserve life. His symbol was the jaguar.

- **Tonatiuh:** Fifth most important deity in the Aztec pantheon. He is the god of fire and sacrifice and was often portrayed as a young man standing on a rock with flames coming out of his head. His name can be translated as "the lord of the feast," and he was considered to be the supreme male deity. He was also called "the god of hidden treasures." His symbol is a flint knife with which he cuts out hearts from sacrificial victims. He was considered to be an intermediary between Xipe Totec and human beings, especially warriors, since it was believed that Xipe Totec could not approach those who had died in battle due to his own status as a victim of sacrifice.

- **Xipe Totec:** The Flayed God, god of vegetation and harvest, and the Lord of the dance. He was believed to be the cause for the annual season changes and one of the four gods responsible for the planting, growing, and harvesting of crops. He is depicted as an old man with wrinkles and flayed skin that he wears like a suit. He carries a yellow disk on his forehead, a black stripe across his chin, and an ear of maize and flowers in each hand. He also appears wearing a large, round headdress as well as other feathered headdresses

- **Xiuhtecuhtli**: Lord of fire and a symbol of the sun, he was often depicted as a fierce-looking warrior wearing armor and carrying a large serpent on his back. In some depictions, he wore a crown of feathers with a red top, symbolizing fire. He was associated with fire, heat, the sun, and lightning, and his symbol is the mamalhuatzin and tecpatl, the two sticks that were rubbed together to light fires in typical Aztec ceremonies. An important part of this deity's worship was the burning of human sacrifices to signify the end of the 52-year cycle in the Aztec calendar and the beginning of a new cycle.

- **Xochipilli:** Prince of flowers, art, and joy, Xochipilli was an important god of the Aztec pantheon. He was known as the Lord of Flowers, and he walked around with a flowery staff. He was depicted as a handsome young man with flowers in his headdress. His power and influence are concentrated in his hands, which are symbols of healing and fertility. To the Aztec people, he was associated with artisans, especially painters and musicians, as well as love, flowers, happiness, and dance. His symbol is painted or carved hands holding flowers or petals growing from them, and he is associated with beauty and creativity.

- **Yacatecuhtli:** The god of commerce, travelers, and merchants, he was said to have invented quipu, a cord-bound Inca writing system. He is usually depicted with an upturned face, big ears, and three diadems on his head. His symbol is a garland of ears of corn, but he is also associated with the cactus, which symbolizes abundance and wealth. Merchants and traders worshiped him during the agricultural seasons as a patron of commerce and trade.

Chapter 5:

Aztec Mythology

The Aztec mythologies were vast and varied, a tapestry of tales that spanned many centuries. Much has been written about these myths, but they are not as well-known as their predecessors, the myths of ancient Greece or Mesopotamia. Myths in Aztec culture were largely based on their belief in the duality of nature, their interpretation of the stars and the sun, the concept of nature as cyclical, and their beliefs in gods and spirits. Themes from one myth often reappear in another, and much about these myths is still unclear, but with the help of researchers, archaeologists, and ethnologists, a clearer picture of Aztec mythology is slowly emerging. The following are some of the most popular Aztec myths.

The Creation of Man

The creation myth of the Aztecs is known as the Legend of the Suns. As discussed earlier, the Aztecs believed that there were four worlds or suns in the past and that we are living in the fifth and final one. This legend of the cosmogonic ages speaks of "suns" that have existed and collapsed in violent ways. During these periods, the creator gods engaged in epic battles, and these fights gave rise to the existence of suns. Four suns have come and gone and were of earth, air, water, and fire. The fifth age is that of the sun of movement (Nahui Ollin), and it began with a sacrifice by the gods, who created it with their blood and gave life to a new generation of humans.

The creation of the fifth sun, the current epoch, fell to Quetzalcoatl and Tezcatlipoca. In this myth, the two gods found the earth totally submerged in water from the deluge that ended the fourth sun. The giant Tlaltecuhtli, a crocodile-like creature, patrolled the seas in search of flesh to consume. It was told that the gods became serpents, went into the sea, and ripped Tlaltecuhtli apart. They threw her lower body upwards to form the heavens and the stars, and her upper body was used to form the land. The back of Tlaltecuhtli sprouted plants and animals, and streams leaked from her flesh. With the earth and heavens in position, gods were ready to create man. Quetzalcoatl was sent to Mictlan, the underworld, to recover the bones of the people who had perished in the fourth age so that they could create man once again and repopulate the new earth. Quetzalcoatl approached the Lord and Lady of the Underworld, saying, "I am searching for the bones you possess. I have arrived for them." Mictlantecuhtli questioned him, "What do you intend to do with them, Quetzalcoatl?" Quetzalcoatl responded, "The gods are hoping that someone should dwell on the earth" Mictlantecuhtli agreed and told Quetzalcoatl to sound his shell horn and walk around his realm four times. But Mictlantecuhtli's horn didn't have any holes. The false conch horn was one of the tricks Mictlantecuhtli used to try to prevent Quetzalcoatl from retrieving the bones. Quetzalcoatl, determined to complete his mission, summoned worms to drill holes in the shell and called upon bees to blow the horn. When Quetzalcoatl heard the horn, he ventured to gather the bones as per his agreement with Mictlantecuhtli, but it turns out that the Lord of the underworld changed his mind. Mictlantecuhtli instructed some spirits to dig a hole and conjure a quail. The quail startled Quetzalcoatl, who then tripped, fell into the hole, and lost consciousness. The bones he had gathered were broken and scattered, and the quail gnawed on them. Quetzalcoatl eventually rose, collected up the bones, and fled from Mictlan. He carried the bones to Tamoanchan, the city of paradise, where the ancient goddess of creation, Cihuacoatl, ground them on a mealing stone and poured the powder into a jade bowl. Quetzalcoatl and the other deities gathered together, spilled their blood over the bowl, and created the first humans of the fifth sun.

The Birth of the Fifth Sun

Now that the earth, humans, and maize were established, the gods gathered at Teotihuacan in the darkness to create the sun. Two deities were chosen to complete the task: Tecciztecatl, a rich and powerful lord, and Nanahuatzin, a weak and poor god. A great pyre was constructed for a fire sacrifice, and the gods commanded that the Lord Tecciztecatl surrender himself to the fire. He tried to do their bidding four times but never followed through.

Nanahuatzin, a frightened man, gathered enough courage to leap into the fire. The flames quickly devoured his body, and his bravery was celebrated. Ashamed of his earlier cowardice, Tecciztecatl then proceeded to jump into the fire. A jaguar and an eagle accompanied him. These animals have then crowned warrior heroes, becoming patrons of the Aztec warriors' orders because of their bravery.

When Nanahuatzin came up in the east as Tonatiuh, the sun god, a great light was cast over the land. Tecciztecatl also rose as he was reborn as a second sun. Concerned that the light would be too intense, the gods threw a rabbit at Tecciztecatl to weaken his light. So, he became the moon and the sun's lesser twin. However, the sun in the sky remained unmoving. The gods dispatched a falcon to question Tonatiuh as to why he remained in place. He replied with a demand; he wanted the blood of the gods. The gods, aware that they must sacrifice themselves to keep the sun moving across the sky, beckoned Quetzalcoatl to perform the deed. Quetzacoatl cut open the chests of the gods and took out their hearts as an offering to Tonatiuh. And so, the sun followed its usual pathway across the sky. As a result, the Aztecs believed that people had to provide blood and hearts to keep the sun going, and the sun would be gone if they didn't sacrifice themselves as their gods did.

Death and the Afterlife

The Aztec's perspective of the afterlife was as complex and diverse as their living world. They believed that their destiny was determined by various factors and took into account many different aspects of a person's life when considering a person's fate in life and death. As much as they could tell, most aspects of their life were strategically planned and carefully orchestrated. The Aztec people were masters at astrology, and using their calendar; they deduced that the date of birth of a person influenced many parts of their life. They could determine personality characteristics, burden and fate, and other attributes of a person by studying the character and nature of their day of birth. Similarly, with the same accuracy, the final resting place for a person's soul was determined by the way they died and the type of work they did during their lifetime. The remains of the dead were sent to be incinerated or entombed so that they may be returned to Coatlicue, the earth goddess. This means that Coatlicue's body was seen as a divine vessel for all the dead, both human and animal. This same attribution was given to her masculine counterpart, the god Tlaltecuhtli, also known as Earth's monster. The deceased's body or the cremated ashes rest in the soil, providing nour-ishment to Tlaltecuhtli and Coatlicue while the soul moves on to a predestined location, depend-ing on the way the individual dies. The Aztecs had a few ideas about these locations.

- **Chichihuacuauhco**

Chichihuacuauhco was also referred to as the Wet Nurse orchard, the orchard of gods, or Tonaca Cuauhtitlan. It was a paradise that received de-ceased children whose innocence had been pre-served as a result of their early death. They died while still drinking from their mother's breasts and so had not yet eaten directly from the earth. This rendered them unsullied and pure; in other words, they did not have any obligations to the gods for the earthly riches they never used. The landscape of this place was abundant with trees, and these trees produced branches that had breasts that produced milk that could be used to feed the little babies. The Aztecs held two views on the souls that occupied this realm. The first theory was that human beings were doomed to extinction, but the children would return from the afterlife to repopulate the world. The second belief was that this was an intermediate place for those children who had died and had not yet been reborn. They would remain in this haven until the day of their rebirth when they would be sent back to earth to begin a new life.

- **Tonatiuh-Ilhuicac**

The souls of soldiers who died in battle and those of mothers who died while giving birth rested in Tonatiuh-Ilhuicac also called the Heaven of the Sun. It was the dwelling place of the Sun and perhaps the most desirable ending for a deceased's soul because it was seen as a place of glory and privilege. Those who arrived here were fortunate enough to witness the sun's daily cycle. The soldiers would go east and trail the sun as it rose through the morning sky; that is when they were not fighting harmless mock battles and singing war chants. It's reasonable to assume then that Aztec soldiers were motivated by the desire for rest and relaxation because they understood that if they fell on the battlefield, they would go to the palace of the sun. The women who died during natural childbirth were sent to Tonatiuh-Ilhuicac, where they were no longer subject to the earth's pains and tortures. Aztecs believed that death during labor was a battle with natural forces and, therefore, an honorable deed. Unlike the soldiers, the souls of the women would go westward to Cihuatlampa, where they would accompany the sun as it set across the night sky. They will carry him on a cloak of quetzal feathers, marching before him, singing praises of his greatness as they guard him in his descent into the underworld. Following four years of happiness and joy, it was believed that these souls would go on to live in the clouds. The male warriors would be transformed into beautiful flying animals that could move freely between the heavenly and earthly realms, while the women became goddesses who could return to their earthly homes to find their husbands.

- **Tlalocan**

This paradise of the rain god, Tlaloc, was a special destination for those specially chosen by him. Aztecs believed that Tlaloc directly orchestrated any death related to water, and it means that such an individual was chosen by the rain god to sit in his paradise and be governed by him. In the Aztec culture, death by drowning or being struck by lightning was seen as a sign that the person would be reincarnated in Tlalocan. Other signs include diseases relating to water or water-based incidents. Tlalocan was also the place where children who had been offered as a sacrifice to Tlaloc were sent to. All who come here are made servants of Tlaloc and are called ehecatotontin (little winds) and ahuaque (Master of Water). The corpses of these people will not be burnt but buried. It was a gesture that showed gratitude to the rain god for providing vegetation and rain. The corpses were believed to be seeds that would later sprout deep within a sacred mountain bringing forth water as clouds, rivers, and streams to feed the earth. This paradise is always in summer and is lush with flowers, vegetation, and streams of milk. Those souls who inhabited this place were extremely fortunate to be guided by Tlaloc, for there was no hunger, no thirst, and no pain in his paradise. Its inhabitants lived in peace and serenity, free from exhaustion or unhappiness.

- **Mictlan**

A black and lurid underworld, Mictlan was seen as the unhealthily dark underbelly of the Earth. It was an area reserved for the souls of everyone else, regardless of status. It was a destination of ambiguity and uncertainty. Individuals who died of old age, accidents, illnesses, or under circumstances not worthy of the other three destinations would go here. It was regarded as a place of misery, death, and fear. The god of the dead and his female companion, Mictlancihuatl, lived there. To reach this dreadful place, the dead were required to undertake a long journey full of perilous natural obstacles. This treacherous passage took the dead through each of the nine underworlds and lasted four years. The first stage is crossing a body of water called Apanohuaya. They would need a dog who had been buried with them to swim across the river. They would emerge from the river completely nude and move onto the next stage, Tepetl Monamictia, a close pair of hearty mountains that continuously clashed against each other. The next stage after that required climbing a mountain called Itztepetl. The surface of the mountain was hard and sharp like obsidian, cutting the soles of their feet as they climbed. This was followed by the next trial that led to eight gorges called Cehuecayan, where the frigid temperatures gave rise to eternal winter, and eight valleys called Itzehecayan, where the murderous winds sliced through their flesh. After overcoming this, they would venture down a path called Temiminaloyan, which exposed them to an unending flow of arrows, and that is when they discovered that a jaguar had consumed their hearts. The next stop would be a mysterious place where the dead would be met with a kind of crocodile or lizard called Xochitonatl. Lizards were symbolic of the earth and were often associated with the end of the year. This symbolized to the dead that their treacherous encounter was nearing an end.

At this juncture, the dead would be required to cross the nine rivers called Chiconahuapan, with the assistance of the Techichi dog, in order to finally arrive at Chiconamictlan, where Mictlantecuhtli will welcome them. This is when the dead finally disconnect from the earth and their physical body, disintegrating and disappearing forever into nothingness and oblivion. There's no chance of eternal life or anything for those who are destined to Mictlan. Immortality was seen as a privilege reserved for those chosen to inhabit the other three realms.

On the other hand, in this lighter interpretation, Mictlan is regarded as a state of "consciousness," attained not through any specific act of death and resurrection but a process of gradual dissolution and development of consciousness. In this view, Mictlan is not a "place" but a state of being, not a condition but a process of self-realization, not a final destination but a process of transformation. If this idea is applied to Mictlan, then it can be perceived to be identical to the state of being between lives or between death and rebirth. The soul's nine-level journey into the realm of Mictlan is symbolic of a reverse journey back into a mother's womb. Like the womb, Mictlan is a place of darkness, warmth, silence, and solitude, where the soul finds itself effectively isolated from all that it has known before. The number nine might also represent the nine missed menstrual cycles during pregnancy, and the struggle might represent the adversities, troubles, and changes of transformation that the soul experiences during the nine-year gestation period.

Conclusion

Aztec mythology and culture are fascinating, entertaining, and informative, a fitting topic for research if ever there was one. Their myths are full of vibrant descriptions of the land they called home and fanciful accounts of their past. Their stories all have the feel of myth to them, even those that are not entirely fanciful. Their culture was one of the most advanced in Mesoamerica, and they had a fantastic sense of aesthetics.

They were an incredibly advanced nation when it came to astronomy and mathematics. They were able to accurately predict eclipses, keep track of the movements of the stars and make incredibly complex calendars using a number system that was beyond anything seen before or since in the Americas. They even invented their own system of writing and made most of their tools and weapons out of bronze, a feat that no other culture in the

Americas would accomplish until more than five centuries after the fall of the Aztec empire.

They were deeply spiritual people, viewing life as a journey or a path rather than an end in itself. This was illustrated by their contemplations on death, reincarnation, and the afterlife. Death was not an abstract concept to them; rather, it was experienced and perceived as a transition from one level of existence to another. They believed that life and death were inextricably linked and the body and the soul were a single entity. Death was an important part of life, as it provided a sense of continuity, action, and meaning. This elaborately constructed cosmology was intimately linked to their daily lives, social systems, and political organization. It was the cornerstone of their existence.

In order to enjoy a good life here on Earth, one had to accept death as part of the cycle of life, viewing it as but a passage from one life to another. This concept of death following a period of renewal is common in the myths and legends that have survived through the ages, showing that the Aztecs saw earthly existence as a microcosm of the universal struggle for survival. This is clearly illustrated by the importance that they attributed to maize, a symbol of life and fertility. The widespread use of maize in their daily lives was seen as a metaphor for the fundamental renewal of humanity, symbolizing rebirth, growth, and the continuation of life. This idea of cyclical renewal also explains how they could so easily accept the periodic return of the same deities or deities with similar or identical attributes.

Life among the Aztecs was experienced as a journey to be undertaken headlong in the knowledge that death awaited them at the end. The descendants of the Aztecs today are no longer the dominant people they once were, but they continue to hold a key place in the history of Mexico and its people. Their legacy has been immortalized by those that came after them, with their fantastic myths and legends handed down through the centuries. We now know them as the Nahuas, and their language today is the most widely spoken indigenous language in modern-day Mexico. Their life and worldview have been documented by ethnographers, archeologists, and historians, and their story continues to be retold and transformed by modern-day Mexicans. They live on as an integral part of the Mexican people's culture, language, and history, and like they always believed, their journey continues.

References

Allan, T., & Lowenstein, T. (1999). Gods of sun and sacrifice: Aztec & maya myth (myth and mankind). Time-Life Books.

The Aztec calendar stone. (2010). Choice Reviews Online, 48(03), 48–1646–48–1646. https://doi. org/10.5860/choice.48-1646

The Aztecs' history, art, and culture. (1988). Panorama Editorial.

Brink, T. V. (2019). Aztec civilization. North Star Editions.

Keen, B., & Brundage, B. C. (1979). The fifth sun: Aztec gods, aztec world. American Indian Quarterly, 5(2), 174. https://doi.org/10.2307/1183763

Klobuchar, L. (2007). History and activities of the Aztecs. Heinemann Library.

Mahoney, E. (2016). Ancient Aztec culture. PowerKids Press.

O'Hea, J. P. (1921). Aztec calendar. Notes and Queries, s12-IX(180), 256. https://doi.org/10.1093/nq/s12-ix.180.256c

Raum, E. (2013). The Aztecs: An interactive history adventure. Capstone Press.

Solis, F. (2004). The Aztec empire. Guggenheim Museum